rest

Leader's Guide

Choosing peace, growth, and learning holy rest.

body + mind + soul

Copyright © 2021 by Amy Eaton

All rights reserved. No part of this publication may be reproduced, stored in a retrieval system, or transmitted in any form or by any means – electronic, mechanical, photocopy, recording, scanning or any other – except for brief quotations in printed reviews or articles, without the prior permission of the author.

Scripture quotations marked AMP are taken from the Amplified® Bible (AMP),
Copyright © 2015 by The Lockman Foundation
Used by permission. www.Lockman.org

Scripture quotations marked ESV are taken from the ESV® Bible (The Holy Bible, English Standard Version®), copyright © 2001 by Crossway, a publishing ministry of Good News Publishers. Used by permission. All rights reserved.

Scripture quotations marked MSG are taken from THE MESSAGE, copyright © 1993, 2002, 2018 by Eugene H. Peterson. Used by permission of NavPress. All rights reserved. Represented by Tyndale House Publishers, Inc.

Scripture quotations marked NIRV are taken from the Holy Bible, NEW INTERNATIONAL READER'S VERSION®. Copyright © 1996, 1998 Biblica. All rights reserved throughout the world. Used by permission of Biblica.

Scripture quotations marked NLT are taken from the Holy Bible, New Living Translation, copyright © 1996, 2004, 2015 by Tyndale House Foundation. Used by permission of Tyndale House Publishers, Inc., Carol Stream, Illinois 60188. All rights reserved.

First Printing, 2021
Printed in United States of America

Cover and interior design: Nani Williams
Editor: Mytra Layne

Author: Amy Eaton, Chattanooga, Tennessee
Website: LeadingfromLight.com

ISBN (print) 978-1-7363419-2-6

Table of Contents

A JOURNEY TOWARD REST
Leader's Guide

Letter from the author....................................1-2

PREPARE
    Preparing to Lead REST as a Group Leader...........3
    The Gift of Partnership............................4
    Meet & Discuss Your Group Plan...................4-5
    Group Structure Options............................8
    Monthly Session Outlines........................9-10

GROUP LEADER RESOURCE PAGES
    Encouragement for Leaders......................13-14
    Seeking & Hearing from God........................13
    Small Group Basics.............................15-16
    Group Sign-Ups: Just Be Faithful...............17-18
    A Prayer for You as You Lead...................19-20

DETAILED LEADER SESSION GUIDE
    Group Member Information..........................22
    Group Schedule....................................23
    Group Supplies....................................23
    Planning Notes....................................24
    Connect & Begin Session........................25-28
    Month 1 Session................................29-32
    Month 2 Session................................33-36
    Month 3 Session................................37-40
    Reflect & Celebrate............................41-44
    Group Leader Reflection 45-46
    Acknowledgements..................................47
    References..48

Hi friend,

I love to host women in my home one-on-one or as a part of a small group. It is such an honor to help women draw closer to Jesus, and my heart soars as we talk about Him and His word! I am so excited for you, because if you have this book in your hands, that means you are going to lead a small group through REST! What a beautiful and holy thing you are showing up to do. I am praying for you that you lean into the Holy Spirit as He leads you along your journey.

REST was originally written for a small group I hosted monthly. We were all tired and didn't have a lot of free space for ourselves in our very busy lives. However, each of us were hungry for more of God, yet keenly aware that the current season of life we were in was requiring a lot out of us.

Knowing the deep truth that we cannot pour from empty cups, and at the prompting of the Holy Spirit, the devotional REST came to life as a simple monthly group study. It was humbling and beautiful to hear the stories of how God was moving in each of our lives through our journey toward REST. There is something so special about pursuing God alongside your sister-friends. So very special!

I have been asked often if this can be completed as a group, and the answer is always a resounding YES! That's how it came to life in the first place! However, as a learning and development professional, I know having a facilitation guide can be very empowering for a group leader. No matter if you've been leading women's groups for years or this is your first time, this guide will help you lead your REST group with much success and ease.

You can connect with me on social media too and reach out with questions. I've been a professional corporate facilitator for many years and have hosted ladies' small groups for many years as well. I'm a small town girl who loves Jesus and the people He places in front of me. It will be my honor to answer any questions you have. I can be found @leadingfromLight on Instagram or Facebook.

You are a beloved and treasured daughter of the Most High God. You can do this! Don't fall into the trap of questioning if you are good enough to lead. I love this quote by Jennie Allen, "Great people don't do great things. God does great things through surrendered people[1]." Just surrender to His lead. He will equip you for every good work, including this here and now. I pray this leader's guide helps build your confidence and comfort as you disciple the women God has placed around you. May you each receive the REST He has planned for you as you walk this journey together.

Peace and rest in Christ,
Amy

Preparing to Lead REST as a Group Leader

Always begin with prayer.

Pray and ask the Lord to give you wisdom and clarity in how to lead and facilitate your group. The resources and tips I provide in this book are simply a guide. I encourage you to tailor REST to fit your needs; it was designed purposefully to be simple and easy to adapt to fit your season of life.

God will equip you for this journey! Here are two powerful reminders from the Bible:

I can do all things [which He has called me to do] through Him who strengthens and empowers me [to fulfill His purpose—I am self-sufficient in Christ's sufficiency; I am ready for anything and equal to anything through Him who infuses me with inner strength and confident peace.] (Philippians 4:13 AMP)

Here is what I am commanding you to do. Be strong and brave. Do not be afraid. Do not lose hope. I am the LORD your God. I will be with you everywhere you go. (Joshua 1:9 NIRV)

Nearly all of the women I meet are busy. This is true for students, career women, stay-at-home moms, entrepreneurs, retirees, and the list goes on. REST is structured with busy women in mind, so that it complements their lives and isn't a stressor. Designed to be a monthly study, it's still easy to adapt it for a weekly or biweekly gathering if preferred. If you decide to lead this group monthly, then you have the option of hosting it three, four, or five months in duration. You can review all of these options in the next section of this guide.

Pray and follow whichever fits you and your season of life right now. God is big enough to bless and use whatever you bring to Him. If you have three months, then that's all you have, and that's enough. If you have five months, go for it. One thing that would stress me sometimes is trying to make the group perfect for the people yet to join.

I learned the hard way the best thing to do is to pray and then set it up as I felt led. I'm telling you from experience: the right people will join if you pray and ask Him to lead them. I promise!

Ever thought of co-leading?

Having a partner to pray with, brainstorm with, and share the leadership burden with is a wonderful gift. Pray and ask God if there is someone you should partner with to lead this study. If yes, pray for clarity and God's will, and then reach out to them to ask if they'd be interested in leading with you. I've occasionally had incognito co-leaders be my helpers. This is someone who didn't want to be listed or announced with the title but served as my brainstorming buddy and helped me in every way. Whether your person is official or under-wraps, if they're along for the leadership journey, here are some talking points for getting started:

✚ *Meet & Discuss Your Group Plan*

Questions to answer:
How frequently will our group meet? Check one:

◯ monthly ◯ bi-weekly ◯ weekly ◯ other _____

How will your group remain connected / feel supported outside of your meetings?

```
NOTES




```

The Gift of Partnership ✚

The Gift of Partnership Cont.

Who owns what and when? To help with roles and responsibilities discussions, consider these questions to get you started:

> Are you rotating who is facilitating during the meetings?

> Will you share the speaking/leading?

> Can you do periodic text check-ins on each member just to say "Hi, how can I be praying with you?" If so, will you split this or rotate it?

> Will you lead a private social media group to remain connected between sessions / communicate?

> Who is responsible for sending out emails, texts, or posts to the group with updates?

The most important thing is don't overcomplicate it, friend.

The above are merely ideas to consider. You can totally just show up to your decided upon location and put out some cheap snacks or water if in person (or tell everyone to "bring your own stuff") and meet/discuss, and then, watch how God leads (I've led a group or a few that way)!

God will ask us to show up and ask us how we'll lead something, even though He knows the answer and how He will provide. I often think about the story in John 6:1-14 where Jesus knew they couldn't feed the masses with their resources on their own. It is like He wanted them to state their lack and trust His abundance and watch Him provide!

You can just show up with your loaves and fishes if that's all you have. It's enough. There is no perfect group nor perfect way to host. As one with professional facilitation experience, my advice is to just think your plans through in advance no matter how simple they are. This will help make your group run smoothly and reduce the stress factor for you.

I've included space for notes throughout this guide, so you can note anything you need to as you go, as well.

**"Are you tired?
Worn out?
Burned out on religion?**

Come to me.
Get away with me
and you'll recover your life.
I'll show you how to take a real rest.

Walk with me and work with me — watch how I do it.
Learn the unforced rhythms of grace.
I won't lay anything heavy or ill-fitting on you.
Keep company with me and you'll learn to live
freely and lightly."

Matthew 11:28-30 MSG

"Rest is where we remember that [God] holds all things together without our help[2]."

-Ruth Chou Simons

"I will give rest to those who are tired. I will satisfy those who are weak."

Jeremiah 31:25 NIRV

```
The below structures are merely suggestions.
I can't reiterate enough that you are welcome to
make this work for you and your season in life.
```

MONTHLY: 3 Months
- Session 1 – Connect & Begin + Month 1 readings & discussions
- Session 2 – Month 2 readings & discussions
- Session 3 – Month 3 readings & discussions

MONTHLY: 4 Months
- Session 1 – Connect & Begin + Month 1 readings & discussions
- Session 2 – Month 2 readings & discussions
- Session 3 – Month 3 readings & discussions
- Session 4 – Reflect & Celebrate!

MONTHLY: 5 Months
- Session 1 – Connect & Begin
- Session 2 – Month 1 readings & discussions
- Session 3 – Month 2 readings & discussions
- Session 4 – Month 3 readings & discussions
- Session 5 – Reflect & Celebrate!

BIWEEKLY
Choose one of the monthly plans, set a start and end date, and plan to meet biweekly. Alternate the "Monthly Session" discussion plans with a "SOAP" discussion, chatting through the SOAP studies you have done for the previous 2 weeks.

WEEKLY
Choose one of the monthly plans, set a start and end date, and plan to meet weekly. Agree on which dates you will focus on your "Monthly Session" discussion plans first. Then, plan to complete and/or discuss the weekly SOAP studies during the other weeks that you meet.

Group Structure Options

Monthly Session Outlines

Note: these are summaries. Details as well as space for documentation and notes are listed in the final section of this Leader's Guide.

> CONNECT & BEGIN

Note: this can be a standalone meeting as your first session together or combined with Month 1 below.

- Welcome & prayer
- Share group details (dates, times, location, leader contact information)
- Read pages 1 – 7 (pre-work or during group)
- Facilitate activity on page 8
- Discussion
- Prayer requests & pray

> MONTH 1: REST FOR THE BODY

- Welcome & prayer
- Read page 9 (pre-work or during group)
- Discuss prompts 1 – 4 on page 10
- Discuss study tools to explore before your next gathering:
- Memory verse listed under prompt 5 on page 10
- Weekly SOAPs
- Monthly reflection on page 16
- Prayer requests & pray

> MONTH 2: REST FOR THE MIND

- Welcome & prayer
- Month 1 reflection discussion (page 16 or thoughts from SOAPs)
- Read page 17 (pre-work or during group)
- Discuss prompts 1 – 4 on page 18
- Discuss study tools to explore before your next gathering:
- Memory verse listed under prompt 5 on page 18
- Weekly SOAPs
- Monthly reflection on page 24
- Prayer requests & pray

CONT. Monthly Session Outlines

> MONTH 3: REST FOR THE SOUL

- Welcome & prayer
- Month 2 reflection discussion (page 24 or thoughts from SOAPs)
- Read page 27 (pre-work or during group)
- Discuss prompts 1 – 4 on page 28
- Discuss study tools to explore before your next gathering (or to keep the individual journey going if you are not meeting after this):
- Memory verse listed under prompt 5 on page 28
- Weekly SOAPs
- Monthly reflection on page 34
- Prayer requests & pray

> REFLECT & CELEBRATE

Note: this is an optional session.

- Welcome & prayer
- Month 3 reflection discussion (page 34 or thoughts from SOAPs)
- Read pages 34-36 (pre-work or during group) and discuss
- Reflect & celebrate: share how God has moved over the last few months
- Prayer requests & pray

```
NOTES



```

Group Leader Resource Pages

"I can do all things [which He has called me to do] through Him who strengthens and empowers me [to fulfill His purpose—

I am self-sufficient in Christ's sufficiency; I am ready for anything and equal to anything through Him who infuses me with inner strength and confident peace.]"

Philippians 4:13 AMP

Encouragement for Leaders

And let us consider how to stir up one another to love and good works.

Hebrews 10:24 ESV

I am so proud of you for taking this leap of faith, and I am cheering you on!! In case you're not sure where to start, I'd love to give a few tips based on things I've learned along the way.

✚ Seeking & Hearing from God

Pray. I know I said this already, but it's worth repeating:

it is always wise to start and end with prayer.

Invite God to invade your plans and lead you according to His perfect design. Long before you even considered it, God had already planned for you to lead your group! (Psalm 139:16) How special is that?!

The Lord is near, He is listening, and He would love to guide you. He has promised us that if we ask for wisdom, He will give it (James 1:5) – so let's ask! If you feel a nudge in your heart to approach your group in a certain way, and you know it's honoring God to do that thing – then do it!

You don't need a sign in the clouds; He's already spoken to you. I think that was a hard thing for me at first, realizing that the still, small voice inside me and the nudges I felt in my spirit were for sure Him.

If you are not sure that you are hearing from Him, you can pray for confirmation. Another thing that I've found to be helpful is to measure it by asking myself these questions:

```
1.    Does this align with God's heart?
2.    Does it agree with His Word? (the Bible)
3.    Does this honor God?
```

I hope those questions are helpful to you too.

If whatever you are measuring against those questions produces a "no," then I caution you to keep praying for direction. Although, I have a sneaking suspicion that your answers to those three questions are going to be, "Yes!"

I used to wrestle so much with the planning of my groups, and I had to finally realize that the Lord delighted in my obedience to say, "yes," to Him. I was often simply overthinking the details. It is Christ who strengthens you (Philippians 4:13)!

Trust that, and keep walking forward.

Small Group Basics

If you sometimes fall into the "overcomplicating things" zone like me, then perhaps some basic planning tips will be helpful as you get ready to lead your group.

The following is a list of helpful questions to explore as you nail down basic logistics.

✤ **Determine the where, when, what, and how of your group:**

Where will you meet: online? (what venue?) in person? (what venue?)

When will you meet: what dates and times work for your study plan and schedule?

What supplies will you need: are you supplying books to your attendees? Notecards or pens? Food or beverages? Childcare?

How will you invite others to join you? Is this a church small group? Will you invite a few select friends or post on social media to gauge interest?

- **WHERE?**

- **WHEN?**

- **WHAT?**

- **HOW?**

Group Sign-Ups

Just Be Faithful

Over the years, I have led groups of women in my home that varied in size from super small to scary big. I've led women's groups via live Zoom meetings and via drop-in-with-a-comment-or-post-whenever-you-have-time-Facebook-groups. I've felt the sting of hosting seemingly unsuccessful groups as well. I still remember the night of a group that not one person came. I was embarrassed and cried my little heart out, although I later realized God still had a special gift in that solo evening…

Here is what I've learned in it all: just show up. Pray, prepare, and show up for whoever God places across the table (or screen) from you. I assure you that if you are praying, then exactly who needs to be present will be there. Jamie Ivey sums it up well: "You're called to be faithful, and God will fill in the rest[3]." Just show up, just be faithful, and trust Him in the details.

I recall one evening I was crushed when all of my group members were texting and cancelling one by one at the last minute. I had prepared food and was so looking forward to hosting them that night. My neighbor texted and told me she was excited to meet and rather than sitting in my pity party, I thankfully saw the opportunity of the one. She was the only one still coming. I invited her to either come over for snacks and study, or since it was just the two of us, we could go study over chips and salsa.

Off to the local Mexican restaurant we went! It was the perfect evening, and because it was only us two, we were able to open up to each other in unique and special ways, and God was so honored and lifted so high that evening. I have tears in my eyes right now thinking back upon the grief and joy that night held.

I can't promise your group will "go off without a hitch" because all groups have bumps along the road. Honestly, I can promise you some things will not go according to plan.

Priscilla Shirer offers fantastic wisdom when it comes to interruptions that will inevitably come as well: ***"Believing that life interruptions—divine interruptions—are a privilege not only causes us to handle them differently but to await them eagerly[4]."***

Whatever is ahead, friend, be faithful in the small and the big. ***Much of your most significant ministry will happen in those tiny circles behind closed doors where no one sees and celebrates.***

Bring your loaves and fishes to Jesus, and let Him do the multiplying. (John 6:1-14)

> ***"Believing that life interruptions—divine interruptions—are a privilege not only causes us to handle them differently but to await them eagerly[4]."***
>
> -Priscilla Shirer

A Prayer for You as You Lead

Father God, you know the heart of this beautiful woman seeking to lead this group for Your namesake. You have numbered her days and know every one of them, including this moment when You planned for her to lead these ladies.

You know her thoughts, and the dreams You have placed within her. You know the design of our minds and how we care about people and their opinions. Help this treasured daughter of yours to know her worth in You.

Help her to see that she has been bought with a most holy price, paid for by the willful and priceless blood of Christ. May she see herself through Your eyes, and lead this group with bold confidence. You are her source and will equip her for every good work to do Your will (Hebrews 13:20-21).

Help her to know that the size of her group does not matter. All that matters is that she keeps her eyes on You and continues to seek You along the journey.

Remind her that when things don't go according to what seemed like the plan, You are always at work in the details – and often especially in our interruptions. May You be glorified in their group's time together, and may they see Your miracles occur.

May they each find the REST You have planned for them and the peaceful refreshing You have already prepared. May they truly lie down in green pastures as You restore their souls (Psalm 23:1-2).

To You alone be all honor and glory, in Christ's holy name, Amen.

You are exactly the right person to lead this group. God has called you to it, and He is delighted in your willingness to serve. When you feel a little inadequate, remind your soul that He is your source.

He will help you.

"The LORD is my strength and my [impenetrable] shield; My heart trusts [with unwavering confidence] in Him, and I am helped; Therefore my heart greatly rejoices, And with my song I shall thank Him and praise Him."
Psalm 28:7 AMP

Detailed Leader Session Guide

To help keep things simple, I have included some space in the following pages for you to document anything you may want to write down.

You may choose to use a smart phone to capture notes or some additional method, so these are optional resource pages.

Group Member Information

Group member names and contact information page

✚ Name: _____ Phone: _____

　　　　Email: _____

✚ Name: _____ Phone: _____

　　　　Email: _____

✚ Name: _____ Phone: _____

　　　　Email: _____

✚ Name: _____ Phone: _____

　　　　Email: _____

✚ Name: _____ Phone: _____

　　　　Email: _____

✚ Name: _____ Phone: _____

　　　　Email: _____

✚ Name: _____ Phone: _____

　　　　Email: _____

group schedule

✚ | WHERE?

✚ | WHEN?

group supplies

Use this space to document any supplies you'll need for your group that you brainstormed previously. A couple options to consider: if you are meeting in person, you could offer your group members 2 notecards per monthly memory verse or have extra pens on hand. A great tip is to think of what you would want/need if you were an attendee. Then, decide is that something you feel led to supply as the leader? You can always encourage them to bring these items as well!

NOTES:
For planning

Connect & Begin Session

Reminder: this can be a standalone meeting as your first session together, or combined with Month 1.

———

"Where there is a lack of rest, there is an abundance of stress[5]..."

-Lysa TerKeurst

———

Attendance:
If you're reporting to your church who attended, and/or you want to remember to check in on people who missed, use this space to document who attended this session.

Welcome & Prayer:
Welcome group members as they arrive, and then, when it's time, begin with a prayer over your session. Pray whatever is on your heart. If it's helpful, here's a simple prayer you can pray:

Father God, thank you for this opportunity to gather as a group. I pray that we honor You fully in our time together and along this journey toward rest. May we each receive from You exactly what You desire. We come with open hearts and hands, ready and hopeful. In Jesus mighty name, Amen.

Consider a Prayer Jar: If you have a large group, and don't have time to take individual prayer needs, consider putting out a prayer jar or bowl and some notecards and pens. Encourage the ladies to fill out a card with a prayer need and drop it in the jar or bowl before they leave.

You can tell them to note it as private if they don't want it shared with the group (this only applies if you plan to send out a full prayer list after each session.) If you plan to take prayer requests, you are welcome to do those now or at the end of the session. I find it is most helpful to host at the end, so that everyone is feeling more comfortable with sharing at that point in your connecting time.

Group details to share with members:
Session dates, times, location, leader contact info, anything else helpful for a new member to know?

Leader Preparation Notes:
Read pages 1-7 in advance, and be prepared with thoughts you may share in case others are not adding to the dialogue when you begin the activity on page 8. Consider having participated in that activity on your own prior to the session as well since you'll be running the music, time, etc.

Facilitate Discussion:
Encourage your group members to share their thoughts, comments, or insights on what you have read together so far and/or do the reflective pause activity. You may have to go first here to break the ice and demonstrate it's safe to be vulnerable and share. If you have a large group, consider breaking off into smaller groups of 3-5 so everyone feels comfortable and has space to share.

Connect & Begin Session

Prayer Requests

You are welcome to lead the prayer requests here if you aren't doing the "prayer jar" approach. Make sure you always offer some space for your group to ask for prayer, whether it is here in this open space before you conclude or via a collection tool like the jar or a group message format. Prayer is the most powerful thing we get to be a part of. Don't skip it!

If you are praying now, you are welcome to ask for a volunteer to lead the prayer. Sometimes I've led and/or been a part of a group where we each prayed for the needs of the person to the left of us.

There is no perfect formula. Just trust whatever God is leading you to do here, friend. And there's no shame or issue with praying with your eyes open as you go through the list you note on the next page.

PRAYER

LIST REQUESTS HERE:

Month 01

This month, let's discuss what the Bible says, and what Jesus modeled about caring for the body.

Attendance:

If you're reporting to your church who attended, and/or you want to remember to check in on people who missed, use this space to document who attended this session.

Welcome & Prayer:

Welcome group members as they arrive, and then, when it's time, begin with a prayer over your session. Pray whatever is on your heart.

Leader Preparation Notes:

Prepare for this session by reading pages 9-11 in advance. Make notes on what you might answer for questions 1-4 on page 10. Make yourself familiar with the SOAP study process detailed on page 11. You'll be encouraging your group to complete the SOAP studies weekly.

Month 01

This month, let's discuss what the Bible says, and what Jesus modeled about caring for the body.

Facilitate Discussion:

> Walk through the question prompts 1 – 4 on page 10 together, pausing for input after each. You may have to go first here to break the ice and demonstrate it's safe to be vulnerable and share.

> Encourage your group members that they can keep their response to question 4 to themselves, sharing it is optional. They can also take an extra day or two to pray about their answer. Some people are quick to answer and others like to take time before they make a month-long commitment.

> For this discussion, if you have a large group, consider breaking off into smaller groups of 3-5 so everyone feels comfortable and has space to share.

Cover the study tools to explore and work through before your next gathering:
- o Memory verse listed under prompt 5 on page 10
- o Weekly SOAPs
- o Monthly reflection on page 16

01

Prayer requests:
Make time to collect prayer requests from your group members. Pray before concluding. There's space below for documenting notes if you're taking prayer requests here:

This month, let's discuss what the Bible says, and what Jesus modeled about caring for the mind.

Attendance:
If you're reporting to your church who attended, and/or you want to remember to check in on people who missed, use this space to document who attended this session.

Welcome & Prayer:
Welcome group members as they arrive, and then, when it's time, begin with a prayer over your session. Pray whatever is on your heart.

Leader Preparation Notes:
Prepare for this session by reading page 17-18 in advance. Make notes on what you might answer for questions 1-4 on page 18.

This month, let's discuss what the Bible says, and what Jesus modeled about caring for the mind.

Month 02

Facilitate Discussion:

> Open the discussion portion of your session with discussing the Month 1 reflection (page 16 or welcome any thoughts to be shared from the weekly SOAPs). If you have a large group, consider breaking off into smaller groups of 3-5 so everyone feels comfortable and has space to share.

> Read the story on page 17 (can be done together or assigned as pre-work. If reading together, you can have someone read it aloud or give a 3-4 minutes to read on their own.)

> Walk through the question prompts 1 – 4 on page 18 together, pausing for input after each. You may have to go first here to break the ice and demonstrate it's safe to be vulnerable and share. Encourage your group members that they can keep their response to question 4 to themselves, sharing it is optional. They can also take an extra day or two to pray about their answer. Some people are quick to answer and others like to take time before they make a month-long commitment.

Cover the study tools to explore and work through before your next gathering:
- o Memory verse listed under prompt 5 on page 18
- o Weekly SOAPs
- o Monthly reflection on page 24

Prayer requests:

Make time to collect prayer requests from your group members. Pray before concluding. There's space below for documenting notes if you're taking prayer requests here:

This month, let's discuss what the Bible says, and what Jesus modeled about caring for the soul (heart).

Attendance:

If you're reporting to your church who attended, and/or you want to remember to check in on people who missed, use this space to document who attended this session.

Welcome & Prayer:

Welcome group members as they arrive, and then, when it's time, begin with a prayer over your session. Pray whatever is on your heart.

Leader Preparation Notes:
Prepare for this session by reading page 27-28 in advance. Make notes on what you might answer for questions 1-4 on page 28.

This month, let's discuss what the Bible says, and what Jesus modeled about caring for the soul (heart).

Facilitate Discussion:

> Open the discussion portion of your session with discussing the Month 2 reflection (page 24 or welcome any thoughts to be shared from the weekly SOAPs). If you have a large group, consider breaking off into smaller groups of 3-5 so everyone feels comfortable and has space to share.

> Read the story on page 27 (can be done together or assigned as pre-work. If reading together, you can have someone read it aloud or give a 3-4 minutes to read on their own.)

> Next, walk through the question prompts 1 – 4 on page 28 together, pausing for input after each. You may have to go first here to break the ice and demonstrate it's safe to be vulnerable and share. Encourage your group members that they can keep their response to question 4 to themselves, sharing it is optional. They can also take an extra day or two to pray about their answer.

Cover the study tools to explore and work through before your next gathering:
- o Memory verse listed under prompt 5 on page 28
- o Weekly SOAPs
- o Monthly reflection page 34

03

Prayer requests:

Make time to collect prayer requests from your group members. Pray before concluding. There's space below for documenting notes if you're taking prayer requests here:

Reflect & Celebrate (optional)

Note: This is an optional session.

Attendance:
If you're reporting to your church who attended, and/or you want to remember to check in on people who missed, use this space to document who attended this session.

Welcome & Prayer:
Welcome group members as they arrive, and then, when it's time, begin with a prayer over your session. Pray whatever is on your heart.

Leader Preparation Notes:
Prepare for this session by reading pages 35-36 in advance. Make notes on what insights you might share regarding your thoughts on rest found in worship.

Reflect & Celebrate (optional)

Facilitate Discussion:

> Open the discussion portion of your session with discussing the Month 3 reflection (page 34 or welcome any thoughts to be shared from the weekly SOAPs). If you have a large group, consider breaking off into smaller groups of 3-5 so everyone feels comfortable and has space to share.

> Read the story on page 35-36 (can be done together or assigned as prework. If reading together, you can have someone read it aloud or give a 4-5 minutes to read on their own.

Reflect & celebrate:
Share how God has moved over the last few months!

Prayer requests:
Make time to collect prayer requests from your group members. Pray before concluding. There's space below for documenting notes if you're taking prayer requests here:

"Those who live in the shelter of the Most High will find rest in the shadow of the Almighty."

Psalm 91:1 NLT

Group Leader Reflection

WAY TO GO!

You just wrapped up leading a group through the REST journey! This is a big deal, and you should celebrate with your co-leader or a close friend! Spend time praying and thanking God for the opportunity and all He has done over these last few months.

While you're at it, take some time to reflect back upon the journey through the prompts below.

✜ What was a big God moment for me during these sessions as the leader?

✜ How has leading this group impacted me?

✚ What did I do well in leading this group?

✚ What would I do differently as a more seasoned group leader?

✚ Anything else I want to note to remember/look back upon?

Acknowledgements

✣ Written by: Amy Eaton

I can't thank my beloved husband enough for the patience and kindness he shows me. He encourages me and supports me in my dreams and the things God stirs in my heart. Justin, I would not be the woman I am today without the love of Christ poured out through you. Thank you for loving me well and encouraging me to answer God's call.

I give all praise and honor to God for anything special about this Leader's Guide you hold in your hand. To Him alone be all the glory for every reader's blessing He creates through this tool. It is He who gave me the vision for it from the start, and without His nearness and guidance, it would not exist. I'm so deeply thankful He led me on a journey to stillness and closeness with Him. What a privilege it has been to help bring this guide and the REST book to you, to encourage you to draw closer, too.

✣ Edited by: Mytra Layne

To Mytra, thank you for listening to the nudges of Holy Spirit, and your obedience to His call and gifts of editing. Thank you for your willingness to share your gift with others to help us present our heart-thoughts with excellence because of your gift of editing. You are a blessing, and I pray God blesses you for your kindness. Thank you for helping me with clarity and using your gifts and passions to serve Him. Love you!

✣ Designed by: Nani Williams

To Nani, you have walked continually through this vision with me, and I am so humbly grateful. I'm so grateful that you and I get to dream together and that you don't run the opposite direction when I start dreaming up lofty ideas – ha! I pray the Lord blesses you for your generosity and kindness. Thank you for saying "yes" to Him as He whispered to you and for being a willing heart. Thank you for using your gifts to honor Him. You make the world a more lovely place with your artistry and excellence. Love you!

References

1. Jennie Allen, Anything: The Prayer That Unlocked My God and My Soul. (Nashville, TN: W Publishing, an imprint of Thomas Nelson, 2011), xii.
2. Ruth Chou Simons, Beholding and Becoming: The Art of Everyday Worship. (Eugene, Oregon: Harvest House Publishers, 2019), 199.
3. Jamie Ivey, You Be You: Why Satisfaction and Success are Closer Than You Think. (Nashville, TN: B&H Publishing Group, 2020), 42.
4. Priscilla Shirer, Life Interrupted: Navigating the Unexpected. (Nashville, TN: B&H Publishing Group, 2011), 28.
5. LysaTerKeurst. Quote from Lysa TerKeurst. Twitter, Lysa TerKerst, 26 Apr. 2018, https://twitter.com/lysaterkurst/status/989671737582342144.

About the Author

Amy Eaton is a proud military wife and a proud military mama. She's a Learning and Development Professional for her day job where she provides employee and leadership development opportunities, coaching, and consulting.

Amy has many years of experience in leading small groups, worship, and other ministry volunteer roles. Her close friends know she's just a simple girl who loves Jesus, the Bible, her family, coffee, and tacos (those last 2 do not go together...but they're both very, very important).

Amy's greatest hope for any project she produces is that people would draw closer to God through her teachings, speaking, and writing. You can connect with Amy to hear her heart, join the conversation on her posts, and/or ask for prayer anytime:

```
Website / Blog www.leadingfromLight.com
Instagram: @leadingfromLight
Facebook: www.Facebook.com/leadingfromLight
Twitter: leadfromLight
```

"Are you tired? Worn out? Burned out on religion?

Come to me. Get away with me and you'll recover your life. I'll show you how to take a real rest. Walk with me and work with me – watch how I do it.

Learn the unforced rhythms of grace."
Matthew 11:28 MSG

You can't pour into others if you are totally empty yourself.

You are worthy of rest, beloved.

REST: Choosing Peace, Growth, & Learning Holy Rest is a simple, yet incredibly impactful 3 month journey designed for the busy woman in mind.

Amy invites you to explore what Jesus modeled and what the Bible teaches us about honoring rest as a holy necessity, worthy of fighting for.

REST can be requested at local book stores via ISBN 978-1-7363419-0-2

REST can also be purchased via Amazon, search "REST: Choosing Peace, Growth, & Learning Holy Rest" in the search field.

Read more on Amy's site at www.leadingfromLight.com/REST

www.ingramcontent.com/pod-product-compliance
Lightning Source LLC
Chambersburg PA
CBHW050746110526
44590CB00003B/96